Unstable Earth

What Happens if We Overfish the OCEANS?

Angela Royston

A+

Smart Apple Media

Published by Smart Apple Media, an imprint of Black Rabbit Books
P.O. Box 3263, Mankato, Minnesota 56002
www.smartapplemedia.com

Published by arrangement with Wayland Books, London.

Cataloging-in-Publication Data is available from the Library of Congress
ISBN: 978-1-62588-162-5   (library binding)
ISBN: 978-1-62588-572-2   (eBook)

Picture Acknowledgements:
Dreamstime: Michael De Nysschen 24, Jvdwolf 26-27, Logray 8-9,
Lunamarina 29m, Paffik 27, Vilainecrevette 11; Shutterstock: AleksandrN
12, alexsalcedo 19b, Andreas Altenburger 10, Lara Barrett 29t, Willyam
Bradberry 15, Jan van Broekhoven 7m, Stephen Bures 14, Rich Carey 6,
Fineart1 19t, idreamphoto 24-25, Tischenko Irina 5, trevor kittelty 16b,
17b, Khoroshunova Olga 23b, Pinosub 13, pinyoj 21t, andrej pol 12-13,
poppit01 16-17, Elzbieta Sekowska 9t, sevenke 4, Alan Smillie 3, 7b, Bjorn
Stefanson 18, think4photop 22b, vichie81 28-29, Christian Vinces 22-23,
Monika Wieland 20-21.

Printed in the United States by CG Book Printers
North Mankato, Minnesota

6-2016

Contents

Plenty of Fish in the Sea?

The oceans are not teeming with fish. Fish tend to gather in some areas more than others. These places, called **fishing grounds**, are mostly in the waters around the edges of the continents where the sea is fewer than 650 feet (200 m) deep. For centuries, people have used boats to catch fish in coastal waters.

Where are most of the fish?

Ideal conditions

Fish thrive where there is plenty of food. They feed mostly on other fish in a food chain that relies on **phytoplankton** – microscopic plants that float on the surface of the water. For this reason, fish mainly keep to the sunlit waters near the surface. Below a depth of about 650 feet (200 m), the water is dark. Only a few fish can survive here and many of them come up to the upper layer to feed.

This Chinese fishing boat is one of many in the Pacific Ocean. Among them, Chinese fishing boats haul in one-third of the world's total fishing catch.

Fishing grounds

Many types of fish like cold water. Some of the most plentiful fishing grounds are in cold waters off the coasts of Alaska, Canada, and Iceland. In warmer tropical seas, most fish are found around coral reefs. Until the 1950s the fishing grounds had plentiful supplies of fish that were easy to catch. Since then, however, stocks have been declining and now many fishing grounds are running out of fish.

A healthy coral reef is home to many different kinds of fish and other sea life. Unfortunately, many coral reefs are being destroyed by fishing and other environmental threats.

NUMBER CRUNCHING

In 2010 a total of 85.3 million tons (77.4 million t) of fish were caught worldwide.

In the western Pacific Ocean, off the coast from South Korea to Indonesia, 42 percent of the total was caught.

In the North Atlantic Ocean, mostly off Western Europe, 13.5 percent of the total was caught.

A further 10 percent was caught off the coast of South America.

What is Overfishing?

Overfishing is when so many fish are caught, there are not enough fish left to replace those lost. Traditional fishing boats catch only large adult fish, leaving the young fish to grow and breed. Now fishing has become **big business**, and the methods used are causing many types of fish to disappear from some fishing grounds.

Which fish are being overfished?

Herring swim in large shoals near the surface of the sea. Although herring are still plentiful, environmentalists fear that more are being caught than can be replaced.

Fish at risk

The most endangered fish are those that people most like to eat, such as Atlantic cod, haddock, and bluefin tuna. The numbers of these fish have fallen dramatically since 1980. For example, Grand Banks off Newfoundland, Canada, used to be one of the most abundant fishing grounds, producing 882,000 tons (800,000 t) of cod in 1968. During the 1980s, the cod catch began to drop and by 1992 there were so few cod, the Canadian government made fishing on the Grand Banks illegal.

Consequences for people

The Canadian government wanted to give the cod time to recover, but 30,000 people who were involved in the local fishing industry immediately lost their jobs. In addition, cod as a source of local food disappeared. Millions of people around the world, particularly in eastern Asia and Africa, rely on fish as their main source of food and income. So if the fish disappear there will be dire consequences for the **traditional** fishing communities.

ON THE EDGE

Scientists rate fish populations from overexploited, or overfished, to abundant. In 2012, the Food and Agricultural Organization (FAO) of the United Nations reported that 30 percent of the world's fishing stocks were overfished. A further 57 percent were fully exploited, which means that they were close to being overfished. Only 13 percent were abundant.

As fishing grounds close to the shore become overfished, fishing boats go farther asea to find fish.

Fishing nets are dragged from the back of fishing trawlers. Smaller trawlers work in pairs, dragging a huge net between them.

Factory Fishing

Large **freezer trawlers** are the main cause of overfishing. Their huge nets are dragged along the **seabed** or through the water to catch vast quantities of fish. The fish are then processed and frozen on board. In just two days, a freezer trawler can catch as much fish as traditional fishing fleets do in a year.

How do freezer trawlers catch more fish faster?

Every last fish

As a fishing ground becomes overfished, trawlers have to search harder for the remaining fish. Freezer trawlers use computers and **sonar equipment** to detect and follow **shoals** of fish. Then they scoop up the whole shoal. Some factory trawlers take in fish from several boats. Large trawlers may unload their catch onto the processing ship and then carry on fishing. Sometimes the processing ship has its own fleet of smaller fishing boats, which keep it supplied.

Large fishing trawlers stay at sea for weeks at a time. This ship is fishing in the icy waters of the North Atlantic Ocean.

Instant fillets of fish

Within hours of being caught, the fish are processed and frozen. First, they are sorted by type and then they are **filleted**, which means that their heads, tails, and bones are removed. The flesh is taken to another part of the ship where it is cut into portions and frozen. The waste is made into **fishmeal**, to be used as animal feed or as a fertilizer.

Most fishing trawlers have sonar equipment. Sonar detects shoals of fish by sending out sound signals and charting their echoes. Echoes from shoals in mid water return quicker than those from the seabed.

NUMBER CRUNCHING

Many factory trawlers are more than 330 feet (100m) long—almost as long as a football field. Their nets are up to 230 feet (70 m) wide and can catch 165 tons (150 t) of fish at a time. The biggest ships can process and freeze 385 tons (350 t) of fish a day—enough fish to feed more than a million people!

Death and Destruction

Freezer trawlers damage more than one or two species of fish. As they haul in their catch, they accidentally net or hook many other sea animals, both large and small. In addition, they damage food chains and entire ocean habitats.

How do freezer trawlers damage ocean habitats?

By-catch

Sea animals that are scooped up by mistake along with a shoal of fish are called **by-catch**. By-catch includes large fish such as yellowfin tuna and sharks. As fish become scarcer, trawlers use nets with a smaller mesh, so that young fish and small fish are also caught. Unwanted by-catch is either treated as waste or dumped, although the fish are already dead. For every ton of wild prawns caught each year, 3 tons of other fish are lost as by-catch.

This young shark has been caught by mistake along with the scallops, prawns, and other shellfish. In a small boat, by-catch can be thrown back to sea alive, but in large trawlers the by-catch is already dead when it is discarded.

Coral reefs have been called the "rain forests of the sea," because they support so many species of sea animals. These delicate habitats are easily damaged by overfishing and fishing equipment.

Destroying habitat

When the vast nets of a freezer trawler scrape across the seabed, they disturb and may destroy the whole habitat. The seabed is a haven for many types of sea creature, particularly young fish and invertebrates, such as sea urchins and starfish. Cod feed on crabs, squid, sand eels, and smaller fish that live on the seabed. Freezer trawlers destroy the food chains and the delicate **ecosystem** on which cod, plaice, and other fish rely.

What happens next?

⚠ Fishing in the area is internationally banned.

⚠ The freezer trawlers move to another fishing ground and start overfishing it.

⚠ It is hoped that fish in the banned area will breed and their population will recover. If the whole habitat has been severely damaged, however, that may not happen.

No More Fish and Chips: The North Sea 2020

It is 2020. The North Sea between Britain and northern Europe is severely overfished. By 2012, 90 percent of Europe's stocks of large fish had been overfished, and in 2016 stocks of cod and herring collapsed. This means that almost no fish remained. Local fishing boats have gone out of business. Cod is now a luxury fish, and fish and chip shops have disappeared.

The harp seal population is dwindling. Carcasses are washing up on beaches. The seals' diet of cod and herring has collapsed and the harp seals are struggling to survive.

What happened?

In 2007, the stocks of North Sea cod fell to an all-time low of 41,225 tons (37,400 t) and attempts were made to conserve them. Countries were given quotas —maximum amounts of fish they were allowed to catch. By 2010, the stocks of cod had increased to more than 55 tons (50 t) and fishermen and governments urged the European Union to increase fishing quotas. Instead of waiting for fish stocks to recover fully, the quotas were increased by too much too fast.

With so few fish in the sea, many useless and abandoned fishing boats lie rusting on the seabed.

NEWS HEADLINES

Why have fishing stocks not yet recovered? Fishermen blame seals and other marine mammals for preying on the remaining fish. **Environmentalists** and scientists say that seals are not the problem and that killing them is not the solution.

The North Sea is a wasteland. A scientific investigation into the state of the seabed has found a devastated seascape with little sign of life. They predict that it could take decades for fish stocks to recover.

A few supermarkets sell local fish such as conger eel, coley, and hagfish. Coley used to be sold as food for cats, however, and hagfish are slimy. Neither is popular with customers.

The last local fishing trawler in eastern England has quit. It has been bought by a fishing museum in Yorkshire. Freezer trawlers have already moved on and are now fishing off the coast of West Africa.

Sea Animals in Danger

Fishermen aim to catch the biggest fish because they sell for the most money. This means that the biggest fish are usually the first to become endangered. Big fish have an important part to play at the top of many food chains and food webs. Their loss affects fish and sea animals below them in the chain.

How are big fish becoming endangered?

Tuna is ready to be sold at a seafood and fish market in Tokyo, Japan. Skipjack tuna live in cool and tropical seas and are smaller than bluefin and yellowfin tuna.

Tuna

Tuna are found in oceans around the world and are one of the world's most popular seafoods. They are so popular that stocks of several types of tuna, particularly yellowfin, bluefin, and bigeye tuna, are now in danger of collapse almost everywhere. Skipjack tuna are still **sustainable**, but only when they are caught on fishing lines, because nets trap endangered species of tuna along with the skipjack.

Top predators

Tuna and sharks are important predators, but up to 100 million sharks are caught worldwide every year, mainly for their fins and as by-catch. Removing a top predator can have a devastating effect. For example, sharks prey on rays, which feed on **scallops**. When the number of sharks off the East Coast of the United States dropped steeply after the 1970s, the number of rays increased. This led to the collapse of scallop fishing.

ON THE EDGE

Fishing trawlers are one of the reasons why all types of marine turtle are now in danger of becoming **extinct**. Although it is forbidden to hunt marine turtles in many areas, turtles are still accidentally caught in the nets of fishing trawlers. Turtles are reptiles, which means they have to come to the surface to breathe in air. The nets stop them from doing that and they drown.

A sea turtle in the Red Sea comes to a coral reef to feed. Red Sea haddock are threatened by fishing boats and nets, which also damage the coral reefs.

Villages Deserted West Africa 2030

It is now 2030. Freezer trawlers and fish-processing ships have overfished the waters off the coast of West Africa and have moved into the Pacific Ocean. Villagers on the coast of West Africa have lost their main source of food and income.

More families are abandoning their homes in Ghana in West Africa. Fish stocks are gone here and the people are desperate.

Consequences

Foreign boats caught large amounts of fish close to the shore, so that all the boats had to fish farther out to sea. This was dangerous for local fishermen because their traditional boats were not designed to withstand the heavy waves. Then, fish farther out became scarce and local people could no longer catch enough to feed their families.

The collapse of the West African fishing industry leaves local people destitute. Fish— their main source of income— has gone and they have nothing to sell. Whole villages have been abandoned as people move into the cities.

Tourists are taking over the coast. Some of the abandoned villages have been rebuilt as luxury holiday homes for tourists. Some fishing boats have been converted into yachts to take tourists to beaches up and down the coast.

Some fishermen are using their boats to carry passengers to Europe. The boats are filled with people who are desperate to find work. Single boats are stopped by European **coast guards**, but when boats sail together many get through.

Fishing boats lie deserted on the beach.

A colorful fishing boat heads out into the waves off the coast of Africa. Traditional boats were designed for fishing close to the shore, not far out in the open ocean.

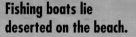

Are Fish Farms the Answer?

People need fish. Billions of people rely on fish as their main source of **protein**, and millions rely on it for their income. The world's population is increasing and so we shall need more, not less, fish in future. If there are not enough wild fish to feed the world, can fish farms fill the gap?

How do fish farms work?

Salmon are being reared in this fish farm in a fjord in Norway. The circles are the tops of pens, or cages, full of hundreds of salmon.

Fish farms

In Europe salmon and trout are among the most popular farmed fish, while carp is widely eaten in China. Shrimp farms are increasing in Southeast Asia. In a **fish farm**, many fish are reared in the limited space of a pen or tank. A salmon farm, for example, may have about 10 pens with hundreds or thousands of fish in each pen. Farmed fish are cheaper to buy than wild fish.

Food for fish farms

Instead of hunting and catching their own food, farmed fish are fed concentrated food. The food is made from wild fish, such as sand eels, herring, and sardines. Each farmed fish eats three to five times its own weight in fish food, which means that the types of fish they eat are themselves in danger of becoming overfished.

The number of sardines in the oceans is increasing. This is because the fish that prey on them, such as cod, are decreasing. Scientists are encouraging people to eat more sardines to restore the balance.

NUMBER CRUNCHING

While the number of wild fish caught in the oceans is falling, the number produced by fish farms is increasing. In 2006, 17.6 million tons (16 million t) of sea fish were farmed, but this had risen to 21.3 million tons (19.3 million t) by 2010. Even so, this was still only one-sixth of the total sea fish. With freshwater fish the opposite is true. About four times as many freshwater fish are farmed than caught wild. Might the numbers of farmed sea fish one day exceed those of wild fish in the oceans?

Many of the fish, such as sand eels, that are fed to salmon in fish farms are also eaten by people. In some places, sand eels are becoming increasingly scarce.

Consequences of Fish Farming

Fish farming pollutes the water around the farms and endangers wild animals that live there. Chile and British Columbia in Canada have large salmon farms. Dolphins, seals, and killer whales were once common along these coasts, but now salmon farmers trap and kill them to keep them away from their salmon farms.

How do fish farms harm the environment?

Pollution

Fish farms produce large amounts of sewage and other waste, such as uneaten food and dead fish. For example, a salmon farm with 200,000 fish produces as much sewage as a town of 62,000 people. The pollution is washed into the surrounding water.

Farmed fish live so closely together that disease spreads quickly from one fish to another. Diseases caused by bacteria and **parasites**, such as lice, move from the pens into the water, infecting wild fish. Fish that escape from the pens also help to spread the disease.

A pod of killer whales swims near the San Juan Islands off Washington State. Tourists come to the islands to watch whales, but the whales are threatened by fish farms, pollution, and the decline in the number of fish for them to eat.

Shellfish farming

Shellfish, particularly prawns and shrimps, are farmed along the coasts of tropical countries in Southeast Asia and South America. The coasts are lined with mangrove trees, which the fish farmers clear away. Shellfish need clean, warm water to survive, but fish farms pollute the water, making it impossible for both wild and farmed shellfish to survive in the polluted waters.

This shrimp farm takes up a large area of a coastal swamp in Thailand. The pollution from the farm seeps into the surrounding swamp waters.

What happens next?

⚠ Mangrove trees are an essential part of the coastal swamps. Wild shellfish and fish breed in the shelter of the trees, and the trees protect the land from storms. When an estuary becomes too polluted for wild and farmed shellfish to survive, the shellfish farmers pack up, move to a clean stretch of coast, cut down the mangrove trees, and start again.

Starving Billions: Southeast Asia 2040

It is 2040. The Pacific Ocean, the biggest ocean in the world, supports the largest fish-eating populations in the world. Fish is high on the menu in China, Japan, and the countries of Southeast Asia. The western Pacific once had the world's largest numbers of fish, but by 2040, fish stocks in the western Pacific have collapsed.

Heavy rain and floods are common now as the world's climates change. Rivers in Thailand burst their banks regularly due to the vast amount of heavy rainfall in the country.

When huge waves batter the coast, the sea floods over the land.

What happened?

When fishing grounds in the North Atlantic and off West Africa collapsed, factory ships moved onto the Pacific Ocean. China, Japan, and Russia on the edge of the Pacific already had their own large fleets of freezer trawlers. They were joined by fleets from Europe and North America. Shellfish farming added to the decline of wild seafood, especially in Southeast Asia.

New mangrove forests are being grown along many coastlines of Asia in an attempt to protect the coast from severe storms and flooding.

The sudden collapse of fish stocks in the Pacific Ocean has pushed most of the world into famine. Now, 85 percent of the world's people do not have enough to eat. The United Nations is urging governments to abandon beef farming, because it takes up huge areas of land that could be used to grow cereals, soybeans, and other basic food.

Few **mangrove** swamps remain in Southeast Asia. Forty years ago, the swamps were full of fish and shellfish, and provided food and income for local people.

In August a **cyclone** moved from the South Pacific and hit Burma with winds of more than 125 miles (200 k) per hour. High waves swamped islands and the coast. The floods reached several miles inland, destroying villages and rice fields. The worst hit areas are those without mangrove trees to protect them.

Children across eastern Asia are suffering from **malnutrition**. Families cannot afford to buy beef and even chicken is expensive. Seafood, once the basis of their diet, is rarely available.

23

Can Fishing be Sustainable?

Overfishing can be stopped and fishing grounds can be protected. The fishing industry could become sustainable, but only if fishing companies and governments work together. Fishing boats could continue to catch fish for people to eat, provided they do not catch too many fish.

How can fishing become sustainable?

Changing the way fish are caught

The fishing industry can protect fish stocks by abandoning large factory ships and using smaller boats. It can stop using huge nets with a small mesh. Increasing the size of the mesh allows young fish to escape. To catch large fish, long lines with hooks instead of nets can be used. This reduces the amount of accidental by-catch.

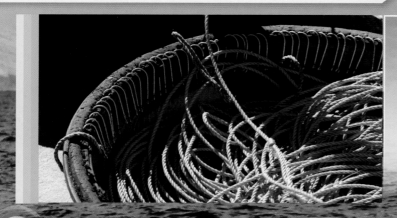

A commercial fishing line is thick, strong, and very long. It is lined with hooks, which are stored around the edge of the container, to stop them becoming entangled.

Many types of whales were almost hunted to extinction, until hunting was banned. Will we be able to save current species of fish before it is too late?

International agreements

Governments have the right to stop other countries' fishing boats from fishing within a certain distance of their coasts. That distance has increased over the last 70 years and has led to several disagreements between countries, particularly between Iceland and Britain.

Cod Wars

In what was known as the Cod Wars of the 1970s, British trawlers refused to recognize Iceland's extended zone, and the Icelandic Coast Guard cut the British ships' nets. Britain sent armed Royal Navy ships to protect their trawlers and there were several clashes between the British and Icelandic ships before agreement was reached.

ON THE EDGE

Until the 1980s whaling boats were allowed to catch as many whales as they liked. Then environmentalists argued that many species of whale had been overhunted and were in danger of becoming extinct. The campaign was successful and commercial whaling became illegal. By 2010 the numbers of some species of whales had recovered, but others had not.

It Can Be Done: Iceland 2050

It is 2050. Iceland has been fishing sustainably since the 1970s. Now its fishing industry is the envy of the world. Elsewhere, the large fishing grounds of the past are overfished and dead, although some countries are trying to protect their sea life.

A naval patrol ship is ready to protect its country's waters from any threat to its fishing grounds.

How Icelanders fish:

A limited fleet of small boats runs on hydrogen fuel, which creates no pollution.

Each boat fishes about four times a week.

The boats use lines not nets.

Each line is about 9 miles (15 k) long and has 14,000 hooks.

Each boat catches about 6.6 tons (6 t) of fish.

The fleet's total catch is enough to feed the local people and export some fish.

NEWS HEADLINES

Early this morning, Icelandic Coast Guard boats intercepted a pirate fishing trawler. The **patrol boats**, which are heavily armed, fired missiles to disable the ship and force it into port. Police have **confiscated** the catch, and arrested the captain and crew.

Around the world, freezer trawlers and large fish processing ships lie rusting and idle. Some have been turned into floating prison ships, but prison guards complain that they smell of fish.

A plague of stinging jellyfish has taken over the coastal waters of the North Sea. Abandoned freezer trawlers are being used to catch the jellyfish. An advertising campaign has been launched in Europe and North America to persuade people to eat more jellyfish.

The jellyfish population has exploded because there are few fish to feed on the young jellyfish. Jellyfish dishes are now on restaurant menus around the world.

Will Fishing Survive?

The glimpses into the future described in this book assume that overfishing and fish farming continue as they are now. However, environmentalists say that the future does not have to be like that. There is still time for governments and **international organizations** to take control and save the oceans' fish.

How can the oceans be saved?

Protecting fishing grounds

Many countries have already agreed to fishing quotas, although campaigners say they are often not strict enough. Inland fish farms are less damaging to wild fish than fish farms in the sea. Freshwater fish farms are more contained and so pollution is less of a problem to wild stocks. Some types of fish, such as tilapia, feed on plants not fishmeal, and so farming them does not endanger other fish.

This fish farm is situated on a lake in New Zealand. Waste from inland fish farms can be treated more effectively so that there is less impact on the environment.

ON THE EDGE

Overfishing is not the only problem that needs to be solved to protect fish and other sea life. Although pollution from factories, **pesticides**, and oil spills poison the seas, **global warming** is the biggest danger. The sea is becoming warmer and more acidic, and this is damaging coral reefs and other sealife. Warmer seas lead some fish to move into new areas where they compete with native fish and disturb existing food chains.

Bluefin tuna are currently overfished and their numbers are dwindling. If enough marine reserves are created, all kinds of fish, including bluefin tuna, could become plentiful again.

Marine reserves

Environmentalists agree that the best way to protect sea life is to create **marine reserves**. These are large areas of the oceans where fishing, drilling for oil, and mining are banned. Reserves now cover 1 percent of the oceans and sealife in them has increased significantly. However, environmentalists advise that up to 40 percent of the oceans need to be protected in this way.

Glossary

big business big companies that control large amounts of money and influence governments and political parties

by-catch fish and sea animals that are caught in fishing nets by mistake

coast guards members of a force whose job is to protect the coast

collapsed (fishing stocks) when fish stock falls to less than 10 percent of its original size

confiscated seized according to the law

cyclone tropical storm with strong winds and heavy rain that begins over warm oceans. In some parts of the world a cyclone is called a hurricane or typhoon

ecosystem community of plants and animals that lives together in a particular habitat

environmentalists scientists who study the environment and work to protect it

extinct no longer existing

filleted when the flesh of a fish is separated from the bones, head, and tail

fish farms places where fish or shellfish are raised in pens to be sold for food

fishing grounds parts of the ocean where there are many fish

fishmeal animal feed made from fish and the parts of the fish discarded during filleting

freezer trawlers large fishing boats that catch huge amounts of fish that the crew sort, process, and freeze on board

global warming an increase in the average temperature of the air at the surface of the Earth

hydrogen fuel the use of hydrogen to produce electricity to power an engine

international organization an organization that includes representatives from many countries

malnutrition condition resulting from a person not eating enough of the right kinds of food for them to grow well and be healthy

mangrove trees that grow in saltwater swamps and along the edge of the coast in tropical countries

marine reserves areas of oceans or seas where sea life and the ocean environment are protected

overfishing when more fish are caught than can be replaced by natural means

parasites animals or plants that live off other animals or plants

patrol boats boats that keep watch over an area of water

pesticides chemicals used by farmers and gardeners to kill animals that attack crops and plants

phytoplankton microscopic plants that float in large masses at the surface of the sea

protein a substance found in food that people and animals need to grow and stay healthy

quota a limited share of a total

scallop an edible mollusk with a ribbed fan-shaped shell

seabed ground below the sea

shoals large groups of the same type of fish that swim together

sonar equipment machine that uses sound waves to detect something that cannot otherwise be seen

sustainable able to be maintained

traditional according to ways and means used for generations

Further Information

Books

Destroying the Oceans: Protecting Our Planet,
Sarah Levete, Wayland, 2012

Oceans: Dolphins, Sharks, Penguins, and More!
Johnna Rizzo, National Geographic, 2010

World Without Fish, Mark Kurlansky, Workman Publishing
Co., 2011

Websites

ocean.nationalgeographic.com/ocean/critical-issues-overfishing/
This website explains what overfishing is and how it
has occurred.

stateoftheocean.org/threats.cfm
Look at this website to find out more about the main
threats to the oceans and what can be done about them.

www.exploringnature.org/db/detail.php?dbID=7&detID=78
This website focuses on what is being done to manage
overfishing in the United States.

Index